T0344010

DIVERSITY
IN SCHOOLS

DIVERSITY IN SCHOOLS

{ Bennie Kara }

SAGE Publications Ltd
1 Oliver's Yard
55 City Road
London EC1Y 1SP

CORWIN
A SAGE company
2455 Teller Road
Thousand Oaks, California 91320
(0800)233-9936
www.corwin.com

SAGE Publications India Pvt Ltd
B 1/I 1 Mohan Cooperative Industrial Area
Mathura Road
New Delhi 110 044

SAGE Publications Asia-Pacific Pte Ltd
3 Church Street
#10-04 Samsung Hub
Singapore 049483

© Bennie Kara 2021

First published 2021

Apart from any fair dealing for the purposes of research or private study, or criticism or review, as permitted under the Copyright, Designs and Patents Act, 1988, this publication may be reproduced, stored or transmitted in any form, or by any means, only with the prior permission in writing of the publishers, or in the case of reprographic reproduction, in accordance with the terms of licences issued by the Copyright Licensing Agency. Enquiries concerning reproduction outside those terms should be sent to the publishers.

Editor: Delayna Spencer
Assistant editor: Catriona McMullen
Production editor: Nicola Carrier
Copyeditor: Christine Bitten
Proofreader: Emily Ayers
Indexer: Adam Pozner
Marketing manager: Lorna Patkai
Cover design: Wendy Scott
Typeset by: C&M Digitals (P) Ltd, Chennai, India
Printed in the UK

**Library of Congress Control Number:
2020945280**

**British Library Cataloguing in
Publication data**

A catalogue record for this book is available from the British Library

ISBN 978-1-5297-1854-6 (pbk)

At SAGE we take sustainability seriously. Most of our products are printed in the UK using responsibly sourced papers and boards. When we print overseas we ensure sustainable papers are used as measured by the PREPS grading system. We undertake an annual audit to monitor our sustainability.

TABLE OF CONTENTS

{ ABOUT THIS BOOK }

Diversity is an urgent topic within education today. In *A Little Guide for Teachers: Diversity in Schools*, the author aims to provide starting points for teachers and leaders in creating a curriculum, either across disciplines or within subjects, that is as deep and diverse as its audience.

- Authored by an expert
- Easy to dip in-and-out of
- Interactive activities encourage you to write into the book and make it your own
- Read in an afternoon or take as long as you like with it!

Find out more at
www.sagepub.co.uk/littleguides

{ ABOUT THE SERIES }

A LITTLE GUIDE FOR TEACHERS series is little in size but BIG on all the support and inspiration you need to navigate your day-to-day life as a teacher.

- ⊕ CASE STUDY
- 🔖 HINTS & TIPS
- 🖋 REFLECTION
- 📦 RESOURCES
- 📋 NOTE THIS DOWN

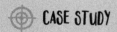

www.sagepub.co.uk/littleguides

ABOUT THE AUTHOR

Bennie Kara is a Deputy Headteacher. She is a speaker, coach and trainer on topics such as language, literature, leadership, diversity, curriculum, assessment and teaching & learning.

She is a Teach First ambassador from the inaugural cohort of Teach First and a Founding Fellow of the Chartered College of Teaching. She has taught English throughout her career in inner city London and South Oxfordshire. She now teaches in Derby.

Bennie can be followed on Twitter on:

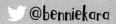 @benniekara

ACKNOWLEDGEMENTS

No book on teaching materialises out of thin air. It is often inspired by conversations between teachers, training sessions attended, arguments on Twitter and most importantly, interactions with young people. There are some people without whom this book would not have come about.

Firstly, thank you to Hannah Wilson. From meeting you at grassroots WomenEd conferences to founding Diverse Educators with you, our conversations have shaped my thinking. Thank you for being my guide and my biggest cheerleader.

To the educators who founded @WomenEd, @BAMEedNetwork, @LGBTedUK and @DisabilityEdUk, thank you for continuing to ensure that our schools are diverse institutions. You do amazing work!

Finally, to Emma Swift. Thank you for the cups of tea, the endless encouragement, and for being generally the best human being I know.

INTRODUCTION

> '*Patience with small details makes perfect a large work, like the universe.*'
> (*Rumi*)

In Indian cosmology, Indra is a divine creator and owner of a net that hangs over his residence at Mount Meru. At each intersection of the net, there is a multifaceted jewel, each reflecting all others. Indra's net is an early metaphor for how the universe is interconnected. When we consider how to create schools that are vessels for knowledge across the world, Indra's net becomes a powerful metaphor for the curriculum of a school in its broadest sense – the intended, the enacted, the hidden and the wider curriculum our students are exposed to.

It is not easy to create a school in which diversity is embraced and embedded in all threads of curricula. It cannot be done by individuals alone. Over the years, valuing diversity as part of school ethos has taken on greater impetus since, at the most simplistic level, educators have recognised a growing BAME population, believing quite rightly that schools ought to be representative of the community. Social change and the greater visibility of marginalised groups means that teachers are engaging in a national conversation about what a diverse curriculum means in practice.

Diversity as a term can be complex and daunting, particularly if your own experiences and educational context places you in a less confident starting position. For that reason alone, it seems important to define the term as fully as we can. A good starting point is its etymology. From the Proto-Indo-European '-wer', we have the Latin 'diversus' which tells us that it means to 'turn different ways'; late 14th century 'diversite' emphasises separateness. In the early 1990s, the word sells the idea of inclusion. In its origins, however, we see the thorny nature of diversity as a term. It indicates a recognition of difference and, perhaps, otherness. It is not a word that levels, or erases.

Perhaps now, more than ever, there is a need to understand how the work we do as educators can mitigate for increasingly problematic national and international narratives on identity. Edward W. Said, in *Culture and Imperialism* (1993: 22), states:

> We are all taught to venerate our nations and admire our traditions; we are taught to pursue their interests with toughness and in disregard for other societies. A new and [...] appalling tribalism is fracturing societies, separating peoples, promoting greed [and] bloody conflict.

This is before we factor in international conflict of the early 21st century, September 11th 2001, the rise of the far right, the emergence of the Black Lives Matter movement and questions of British belonging in Europe.

To be clear, this book defines diversity as inclusive of narratives on age, disability, gender, race, sex, and sexuality. There will be readers who spot that there are characteristics, protected by the Equality Act 2010, that are not listed here, or discussed in full; this is simply a constraint of what can be addressed in schools effectively by individual teachers or in this book. It is, quite simply, a starting point for the classroom teacher.

CHAPTER 1
WHY IS LANGUAGE IMPORTANT IN CREATING DIVERSE SCHOOLS?

This chapter covers:

- Histories, controversies and trends in the language of diversity
- How to navigate the terminology of diversity and inclusion
- How to embed the terminology of diversity in your classroom.

BAME AND PoC

Acronyms are standard fare in schools. When navigating the terminology of diversity and inclusion, terms associated with race and racial identity are awash with acronyms. Not everyone knows, or fully understands, the implications of the language we use around race, and, indeed, the very terminology can feel like a minefield.

BAME stands for Black, Asian and Minority Ethnic. At the point of writing, it is the most widely used acronym for ethnicity in the UK, used officially and unofficially as a catch-all for minority groups. Its UK predecessor was BME; however, it has fallen out of use due to the omission of 'Asian' as a category. BAME, whilst used heavily in the UK, has also faced criticism as it lumps together groups that are not a homogenised mass and does not explicitly include those of Gypsy, Roma, or Traveller heritage. Alongside this, the 'Minority Ethnic' label has raised concern as it diminishes the status of those whose race actually forms a global majority.

'No one today is purely one thing. Labels like Indian, or woman, or Muslim, or American are not more than starting-points, which if followed into actual experience for only a moment are quickly left behind.'
Said, 1993: 433

Internationally, particularly in the US, the acronym 'PoC' is widely used, standing for People of Colour. As a term, it encompasses anyone who is not considered 'white'. It is a much older term than some might imagine, in usage as far back as the 18th century. A variation of PoC is BIPOC (Black, Indigenous, People of Colour), used predominantly in the US again. It is a term that is gaining traction due to the efforts of The BIPOC Project, an organisation that seeks to undo 'Native invisibility, anti-Blackness, dismantle white supremacy and advance racial justice' (The BIPOC Project).

None of these terms comes without criticism. The important thing to note here is that there are widely accepted terms used in the UK and the US to define racial groups. As educators, it is a good idea to keep up with what terms are used, their main benefits and criticisms, and crucially, how and why terms change, are discarded or fall out of use. If you are not sure what someone wants to be called, just ask.

RACE AND ETHNICITY

The history and development of the term 'race' and 'racialisation' is far too huge a subject to do justice to in this section. For the teacher, it is imperative that we understand the difference between 'race' and 'ethnicity'. In sociological parlance, 'race' historically describes a set of biological markers; however, over time, the biological concept of race has been replaced with the idea of race as a social construct. Sociological treatises on the subject are fascinating, as is tracing the trajectory of 'race' as a defining feature. The history of 'race' as a concept can make for some uncomfortable reading – start with Johann Friedrich Blumenbach, go through the problematic Arthur De Gobineau, move on to Franz Boas and Ashley Montagu to get a sense of how the concept of 'race' has altered over time in anthropological circles – then read through Reni Edo Lodge and Adam Rutherford. It is a discourse that makes for uncomfortable reading at times, but embracing that discomfort is part of the process of learning.

'Ethnicity' is a term that is used to describe the cultural identity of groups of people. While 'race' has been seen as a fixed marker of identity in the past, 'ethnicity' is seen to encompass the culture, traditions and social identity of groups of people. It is seen as something learnable, less fixed, more mutable and inclusive of language and style of dress. It can be defined in sub-categories like ethno-linguistic (shared language), or ethno-religious (shared religion). Ethnic theory is predicated on race being a social construct and stems very much from post-Second World War sociological discourse.

For your classroom and your school, knowing the difference is essential. Teaching your students about the difference is equally valuable. Our students have received notions of race, racial identity and ethnicity; in order to challenge their assumptions, particularly on the 'race as biological' argument, we need to know and be able to articulate the difference.

HINTS & TIPS

Teaching students about the language of diversity would make a useful sequence of learning in PSHE. Once you have a grasp of the language of diversity, ensure that your students have a good working knowledge of how language can define, erase, problematise, stigmatise and celebrate difference. Use images to elicit initial responses about how we label people, ask students to identify how difference is labelled in the playground and at home, provide mini-histories of terms with their advantages and disadvantages, and read articles about specific terms to show students how powerful language can be and how changing the way we describe people can lead to a more inclusive society.

DISABLED AND PEOPLE WITH DISABILITIES

Terminology associated with disability has also changed over the years and is immeasurably less offensive than it was previously. Dr Douglas Baynton (1998), a renowned scholar of the history of disability, writes about the term 'handicapped' as originating from a game called 'Hand in Cap' and later on, a method of slowing down horses in a race by weighting them with stones. It is sometimes associated with begging (cap-in-hand); however, this is not generally thought of as an accurate etymological explanation for the term as linked to disability. Despite the fact that it is now widely considered offensive, it is still in use internationally, albeit unofficially.

Language around disability is nuanced and, like race and sexuality, is often self-determined. Some people prefer to use terms that place the person first (person with cerebral palsy, or person who uses a wheelchair) to show that the disability is not their defining feature. The term for prejudice against people with disabilities can be either termed 'disablism' (discriminating against people with disabilities) or 'ableism' (actively discriminating towards people who are able-bodied).

Take some time to read the discussions about the language of disability online. The history of disability is fascinating and makes for some harrowing realisations about historical perceptions on bodies and their social value.

 **REFLECTION**

How often do you challenge disablist language in school?

Increasingly, we are becoming aware of how language discriminates when it comes to disability, for example, do you group people together as *'the* disabled'? Do you say that an individual is *'suffering* from paralysis'? Do you describe a wheelchair user as *'confined'*?

It is easy to feel like you might get it wrong when it comes to language use around disability, but awareness of how language impacts on the identity and worth of a person with a disability can make a huge difference in creating an inclusive environment at school. If you have students with disabilities, and you are unsure of how to create a sense of inclusion in the language you use, ask the student what they would prefer.

LGBT(QIA)+

When describing sexuality, terminology is as varied as the full spectrum of sexuality itself. The terminology around sexuality is rapidly changing in a climate of wider social acceptance and celebration of non-heterosexual relationships and culture. 'Homosexual' was widely used as a pathological definition in psychology and is less common in usage than it was in the mid-20th century. This is a clear example of how language carries implications that we do not fully understand in the moment, and it is only in hindsight that we recognise the problematic implications of defining people in a particular way. The acronym LGBT (Lesbian, Gay, Bisexual and Transgender) began life as only LGB in the mid 1980s, when transvisibility was limited. Through the late 1980s and into the 1990s, the 'T' was added to encompass the Transgender community. Since then, emerging awareness of sexual identity has contributed to the expansion of letters in the acronym; it is worth knowing their significance to avoid erasing these identities completely. The '+' allows for an inclusivity, to take into account the vast spectrum of sexuality:

- Lesbian

- Gay

- Bisexual

- Transgender

- Queer/Questioning

- Intersex

- Asexual

- Non-binary

- Pansexual

 ## HINTS & TIPS

If you want to challenge and support the language used in reference to diverse identities, it is worth doing some pre-reading. Knowing a brief definition of these terms is a starting point for understanding the identities of your students. The generation in our classrooms is more exposed to the language of sexuality than most of their teachers and may feel more at ease defining themselves using some of the terms above. A great starting point for understanding queer history is

Queer: A Graphic History by Meg-John Barker and Julia Scheele. Matthew Todd's *Pride* is a beautiful book that outlines gay history from the mid-20th century onwards. If you want to delve straight into LGBT issues in schools, then I would thoroughly recommend Shaun Dellenty's *Celebrating Difference: A Whole School Approach to LGBT+ Inclusion*.

NEURODIVERSE AND NEUROTYPICAL

It is pleasing to see that diversity of neurological processing in schools is being recognised. The catch-all term used is autism; however, it is important to note the diversity of experience within that term. The National Autism Society provides guidelines when choosing language about autism. It is more widely accepted to use Autism Spectrum Condition (ASC), rather than Autism Spectrum Disorder (ASD), as 'disorder' carries strongly negative connotations.

Another term gaining traction is 'neurodiverse'. This term has gained popularity as a celebration of difference. It goes hand in hand with the term 'neurotypical', for those who are not on the autism spectrum, without using the word 'normal', with its heavily judgemental connotations.

 IDEAS FOR THE CLASSROOM

Neurotypical and neurodiverse are terms that students can explore. One of the best ways to do this is through literature and purposefully incorporating neurodiversity through books, either as class readers or as wider reading. The list below is a starting point:

- *The Curious Incident of the Dog in the Night-Time*, Mark Haddon

- *How to Look for a Lost Dog*, Ann M. Martin

(Continued)

- *Mockingbird*, Kathryn Erskine

- *Memoirs of an Imaginary Friend*, Matthew Green

- *Marcelo in the Real World*, Francisco Stork.

Take a look at the terms used about neurodiversity with students before you start reading, and explore how language conveys thought. Mark Haddon is particularly masterful in omitting adjectives to convey the very factual process of his protagonist's mind. Going further, you could assess based on responses to questions such as: 'How does Haddon use language to explore his neurodiverse characters?' and link to assessment objectives on language analysis.

EQUALITY AND EQUITY

Knowing the difference between those terms is a brilliant starting point for teachers who wish to model diversity in the classroom. It is with this in mind that the individual teacher has to know the difference between equality and equity. The former teaches that everyone is the same. The latter acknowledges different starting points and asks society to create better stepping stones to successful futures.

 CASE STUDY

At a school in South Oxfordshire, students were presented with a story demonstrating the difference between equity and equality. Their English teacher taught students the difference between the two words using a short story about two boys with different physical characteristics being able to complete the same manual labour job. One boy was not physically able to keep up through no fault of his own.

In the end, his companion recognised his need and provided him with the equipment he needed to be able to compete. In an assembly presented by the student council, the students themselves explained the importance of knowing the difference without being prompted. It was a powerful moment. It became part of their language and understanding of the world.

NOTE IT DOWN

OUR OWN UNDERSTANDING OF THE LANGUAGE OF DIVERSITY IS
CRUCIAL IN BUILDING INCLUSIVE SCHOOLS. THIS IS A CHANCE
FOR US TO REFLECT ON OUR UNDERSTANDING OF TERMINOLOGY.

	Reflection – how confident are you in this aim and why/why not?	Action – what actions can you commit to in order to better meet this aim?
I understand the variety of terms used to describe race and ethnicity in the UK and internationally.		
I know how to explain the history of terms related to LGBT status and their cultural significance.		
I can explain the variations in language associated with disability.		
I am able to explain and demonstrate the difference between equality and equity.		

(Continued)

I can challenge
prejudiced language
by teaching about its
nuances.

I could teach a lesson on
language and diversity if I
was asked to.

CHAPTER 2

HOW CAN WE MODEL RESPECT FOR DIVERSITY OF IDENTITY IN SCHOOLS?

This chapter covers:

- The importance of learning together about cultures and histories
- How to model respect for cultural differences, starting with diversity of name
- How bringing your authentic self into the room can start the discussion on diversity.

THE POWER OF NAMES

Uzoamaka Nwanneka Aduba is an American actress whose story about the importance of pronouncing names correctly is a powerful message to students and educators everywhere. In 2014, she explained why she would not exchange her Nigerian name for any other:

> My family is from Nigeria, and my full name is Uzoamaka, which means 'The road is good.' Quick lesson: My tribe is Igbo, and you name your kid something that tells your history and hopefully predicts your future. So anyway, in grade school, because my last name started with an A, I was the first in roll call, and nobody ever knew how to pronounce it. So I went home and asked my mother if I could be called Zoe. I remember she was cooking, and in her Nigerian accent she said, 'Why?' I said, 'Nobody can pronounce it.' Without missing a beat, she said, 'If they can learn to say Tchaikovsky and Michelangelo and Dostoyevsky, they can learn to say Uzoamaka. (Soroff, 2014)

On talking to students now, I hear countless times that teachers have mispronounced names that are deemed difficult because they are not traditionally British names. It is not the first mispronunciation that stays with the student; it is the failure to learn how that name is pronounced and then use it correctly on the second, third, fourth attempt. The unfortunate consequence, witnessed first-hand, is that students with names from different backgrounds start to hide their names. Their pride in their own heritage is eroded. And so they ask to be called something else. They ask to be called 'Zoe'.

It is the very least we can do for our students from diverse backgrounds to learn how to pronounce their names. Take the student to one side when convenient and explain that you want to know how to pronounce their name; apologise for getting it wrong if you need to. Tell them that their name is important – it is who they are and represents the history of their culture. If they say: 'just call me John', explain that their names are important. By erasing a name, we erase that child's culture and background. We tell them that John, or David, or Susan, or Jane, is better suited here.

BUT MY NAME IS JOHN

Modelling your own personal diversity can come in lots of forms. You might feel that your own name and background does not hold relevance for your students from different cultures. Exploring names across cultures is an easy way to show that all names are valuable because they carry a history. Take John as an example. It is a name that transcends cultures. In Hebrew, Yohanan. In Assyrian and Syriac, Younan/Youkhanna. In Romance Languages, Giovanni. In Portuguese, Joao. In French, Jean. In Germanic languages, Johan, Jens, Hans. In Celtic languages, Ieuan, Ifan, Iwan, Ioan, Iain. In Slavic languages, Ivan, Jan. In Albanian, Xhon, Jovan. In Arabic, Yahya (often associated with John the Baptist, a prophet in Islam). The list of feminine forms is just as extensive. If you are a Hannah, you are a John. If you are a Janet, you are a John. If you are a Jean, a Johanna, a Gianna, a Yohana, an Ivana, a Sinead, a Siobhan, a Jane, Juana or a Janice – you are all a John. You are connected to the ancient Hebrew world.

The connectedness of a name can bring worlds together. A teacher making time to explore how the names in the room are linked is a powerful message for students. We value your heritage. Your heritage is important. And it is part of a global network of heritages that we share.

LEARNING ABOUT DIFFERENT CULTURES

Often teachers feel that they will make mistakes when learning about or discussing diversity in the classroom. But the endpoint of showing students that you are a citizen of the world, that you are interested in difference, is that your students feel known. Through feeling known, even to the slightest degree, students feel their culture is valued.

 ## IDEAS FOR THE CLASSROOM

Diversity starts with awareness. Creating a cultural calendar with your tutor group is a wonderful way of raising awareness of

(Continued)

different cultures, identities and religions. Try to include the major religions, but to raise questions about the unknown, including lesser known cultural celebrations such as Holi, World Braille Day, Samvatsari, International day of the World's Indigenous Peoples. You can find an excellent calendar to inspire the process at www. cipd.co.uk/ knowledge/fundamentals/relations/diversity/calendar.

If you teach in an inner-city school, or in any school where students come from a range of different backgrounds, you may be unfamiliar with the contexts and cultures of those students. You may be thinking: 'how can I possibly become an expert in every child's culture?' Unfortunately, learning even one thing about a child's cultural background is an enormously underrated part of our job. When I started teaching, I knew next to nothing about most things. I was placed in East London, possibly one of the most multicultural areas in the UK. I knew a little about Pakistani and Bangladeshi culture having grown up in Leicester. But I didn't know about the range of cultures from Africa, other than what my parents had taught me about Kenya and Uganda – and even then, through the lens of expulsion from those nations. I had to proactively learn the cultural differences between Nigerian students and Ghanaian students – why? Because I was teaching them, and they were not a homogeneous group of students I could label as 'African'.

My lack of knowledge was embarrassing, but I wanted to know the basics. What languages were spoken in Nigeria and Ghana? In my naivety, I quickly learned some key information and felt utterly pleased with myself about doing so, until I reached my English lesson later that week. We were studying Poetry from Different Cultures and I was explaining the similarities between Pakistani and Gujarati culture. In a fit of newly acquired smugness about my cultural awareness, I said: 'In many ways, India and Pakistan have a lot in common. For example, the food is very similar. Like in Nigeria and Ghana, both countries eat jollof rice.' My Nigerian and Ghanaian students were up in arms. Jollof rice, as I learned that day, is a contentious issue between the two countries! What is important to note here is that my students didn't mind me making the mistake because I went on to ask them what I needed to know.

As teachers, we are told to get to know our students so that we can cater for their academic needs. Getting to know students' cultures is equally as important. It needs to be an explicit, visible process. This way, we can model how to investigate, question, learn and grow in understanding of other cultures.

 ## IDEAS FOR THE CLASSROOM

When getting to know a new class, or your registration group, try a deeper version of a 'getting to know each other' exercise. Instead of just asking for names and interests, provide a structured activity where you ask about birthplace, parental birthplace, countries of origin, major foods and cultural festivals. Create a global board and pin their 'places' up publicly on a map. This can be used as a springboard towards deeper understanding of global movement.

If your students are from the same ethnic group, it is equally important that they understand the details of another culture to demystify it. Our students carry misconceptions about other cultures. A nice activity in tutor periods is to introduce 'students' from around the world and ask your class to learn about their culture, their experiences, their food and dress. It is important to focus on the positive aspects of global cultures and avoid 'victim narratives' or surface wealth comparison. Another way to experience lives outside of our own is to collaborate with Lyfta, who provides CPD and an online immersive storytelling platform where students can access a diverse array of real life stories from across the globe (lyfta.com).

LEARNING ABOUT IDENTITY AND MIGRATION

Ruth Benedict, born in 1887, was one of the pioneers of ethnology, a branch of cultural anthropology that identifies similarities between cultures. Both she and Franz Boas ascribed to the belief that no culture is above any other. They are simply different. In *Patterns of Culture* (1934), Benedict outlines the cultural relativism of different societies. Whilst it remains a book very much of its time, the concept she, Boas and later Margaret Mead all advocated was the inter-connected nature of cultures, without singular dominance.

> *'You are the hybrids of golden worlds and ages*
> *splendidly conceived.'*
> Aberjhani, 2009: 66

Powerful stories create powerful identities. When talking about origins, it is useful to remind students of the inter-connected nature of ethnicity and culture. One might start with the story of migration – ancient and modern. A way in might be through the fascinating and student friendly website www.ourmigrationstory.org.uk. Referencing the invasion narratives of the British isles is a good starting point. It would be possible from there to discuss where the invading forces originated. Where did northern and western European peoples originate? What is the cultural connection between north western Europe and the steppes of Asia? How far across the globe can we track our ancestry? How did people get to the Americas?

You might be thinking that there is no way that you can absorb the entire history of global migration in order to show students their connection to the rest of the world. The important thing here is to learn a little before the students, and then to learn with them.

A simple way of showing your understanding of global cultural connections is in having a basic understanding of how language has migrated and is connected. Referencing how our very language is a product of global culture and history starts to bleed power from the utterance 'speak English in England', so often heard by BAME communities as a reprimand. Not only this, but learning a little about languages can go a long way in making students feel valued. When English is the language of global communication, it is imperative that we celebrate the interconnectedness of English with other languages so that we can all feel 'at home' in the words we use.

The key learning point is that language does not exist in isolation. Our words are a product of the world around us, and not exclusively English.

 ## IDEAS FOR THE CLASSROOM

Do students know how language is connected? This short activity can start the thinking process about how languages evolve and tell a story (see Table 2.1). Look up the Latin and Sanskrit versions of these common English words.

Table 2.1

English	Latin	Sanskrit
Candle		
Mother		
Dental		
Vomit		
Orange		

BEING YOURSELF

Teachers fear to disclose parts of themselves because there is a perceived lack of professionalism in doing so. However, there are benefits to controlled and appropriate self-disclosure. In 1971, Sidney Jourard wrote extensively about the relational benefits of self-disclosure, calling it 'the act of making yourself manifest, showing yourself so that others can perceive you' (1971: 17).

With disclosure, teachers must consider some important checkpoints, if sharing with students:

- Does it create common ground without being inappropriate?

- Does it alleviate angst without being inappropriate?

- Does it model a learning journey without being inappropriate?

- Does it address misconception and/or prejudice without being inappropriate?

- Does it fall within the guidelines, written or implicit, of your institution?

Students love to know about their teachers. The interactions you have with your students can be pivotal moments in which you can change their view of themselves and those they perceive as different from them. Whether you class yourself as part of the global majority or minority, your experiences and thoughts as a human being are a valuable part of educating students. Take my experiences in being diagnosed with mild to moderate hearing loss. I went to the doctor and mentioned my struggles with hearing. I was assessed and diagnosed very quickly and given a hearing aid.

When I returned to work the next day, I explained the diagnosis to my headteacher at the time. She could see that I was struggling to define myself now as someone who had a hearing impairment and that I was debating whether I wanted to wear a hearing aid. She paused thoughtfully after I had explained. 'How many students do we have with hearing impairments?' she asked. I counted four in my head and said so. She continued: 'Imagine what it might feel like for them when they see you wearing one.'

 ## REFLECTION

How often do you consider how your own identity impacts on your students' experience of the world?

She was right. I had contemplated not wearing one out of fear that people might perceive me differently. That was the opposite of being myself. It was also a denial of one of the facets of my own diversity. I put my hearing aid in. The bridge built for my students with hearing impairments was clear to see.

When we bring our own backgrounds, experiences, cultures to the table, our students see the world before them. Are you the descendent of Irish migrants? Do you have a disability, hidden or otherwise? Does your family come from somewhere other than this town? How many languages can you speak? What are the dialect words that you love? Who is married to whom in your family? Do you know people in same-sex relationships? Are you in one yourself?

The last question is tricky. It is absolutely clear that no one needs to come out at school if they do not feel comfortable or safe doing so. Some teachers have spoken to students about being LGBT+; that is a choice entirely reserved for the individual. There is no denying that when a teacher is comfortable and safe enough to come out, the effect can be phenomenal for our students.

 ## CASE STUDY

In 2010, David Weston, the CEO of the Teacher Development Trust, tweeted about disclosing his sexuality to students. It went viral when he shared the response he received from a former student. The note said:

Hi David

I know you probably won't remember me, but when I was in Year 7 (2004), you were my deputy form tutor, and I was in sixth form during your 2nd stint at Watford Grammar.

I just wanted you to know how inspirational your assembly was, and how much of a positive impact it had on the

(Continued)

school. I am a heterosexual man myself but have always been proactive in the fight against homophobia.

I know this message may seem a little pointless but I really felt you should know you challenged the ignorance of so many people that day, and if every gay teacher shared your courage, then the world would be a much better place – not just for gay men, but for all of us. For that, I thank you.

They may not quite have had the wherewithal to tell you so, but so many students had so much respect for what you did – never had we witnessed a teacher perform so honestly the act for which they were employed – the act of teaching.

I will carry the memory with me for the rest of my life. Thank you.

NOTE IT DOWN

MAP OUT YOUR AWARENESS OF CULTURAL, RACIAL, GENDER-BASED AND PHYSICAL IDENTITIES. YOUR OWN IDENTITY IS YOUR COMFORT ZONE. ONCE OUTSIDE OF THAT CIRCLE, WE NEED TO LEARN ABOUT OTHER IDENTITIES, IN THE CLASSROOM AND IN OUR LIVES. NOTE DOWN THE VARIETY YOU EXPERIENCE AND THE IDENTITIES YOU HAVE VERY LITTLE KNOWLEDGE OF. COULD YOU ANSWER QUESTIONS AND ADDRESS MISCONCEPTIONS ABOUT THOSE IDENTITIES? MAKE A PLAN TO FIND OUT ABOUT IDENTITIES YOU ARE LESS FAMILIAR WITH SO THAT YOU CAN BE PREPARED FOR YOUR STUDENTS TO ASK QUESTIONS.

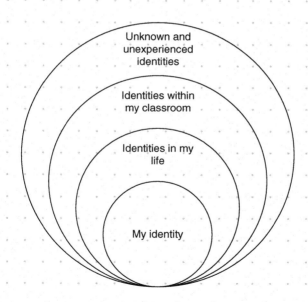

CHAPTER 3
HOW CAN WE CREATE A DIVERSE CLASSROOM?

This chapter covers:

- How to create culturally connected spaces so that we avoid tribalism
- How to ensure that we consciously cater for all voices
- How we can ensure inclusive environments for those with hidden disabilities.

I like the term 'culturally connected' much better than the term 'multicultural' as the latter has taken on negative connotations, thanks to critical media debate labelling multiculturalism as a failure. For me, it is imperative that as educators, we understand the nature of true cultural connection. In 2012, I wrote a blog post about how racial divides become entrenched in schools; students gravitate to those they perceive to be most like them. In that article, I cited comments by David Levin, the then Head of City of London Boys' School, as an indicator of increasing social segregation. He stated that society was 'sleepwalking towards Johannesburg' (cited in Wright, 2012). While there is nothing inherently wrong in students taking the path of least resistance in finding common ground with other students at school, if we want to build societies that have some sense of community cohesion, we can start to make a difference in our own classrooms.

A culturally connected classroom acknowledges the multiple identities in the room. It is an actively constructed entity designed to create cohesion and understanding. It is a conscious space in which students are made aware of difference and similarity, equity and respect.

A SEATING PLAN IS NOT JUST A SEATING PLAN

Picture this. I am observing a Year 11 lesson. Students file in and gravitate to their seats with 'perfect' behaviour. I observe the teaching and progress, duly making notes. Something is strange about this room – something that does not sit right. It occurs to me right at the end of the lesson. Students have been allowed to sit wherever they like and they have chosen to sit in racial groups, most probably unconsciously. I do not believe for a second that these students are racist, or that they have any objection to sitting with peers of a different background.

> '*Diversity is having a seat at the table, inclusion is having a voice, and belonging is having that voice be heard.*'
> Fosslien and Duffy, 2019

In her seminal work of 1997, *Why Are All the Black Kids Sitting Together in the Cafeteria?*, Beverley Daniel Tatum points out that if you walk into an elementary/primary school setting, children of different backgrounds are more likely to be seen sitting together. This changes as they grow older. Tatum proposes that the structural and institutional racism that students of colour face leads to a self-imposed tribalism. Strength and safety in numbers, perhaps. An interesting question to ask ourselves as educators is whether our penchant for grouping students by ability multiplies this tribal effect.

If you work in a multicultural school, by creating a seating plan, we as teachers can move towards mitigating early racial tribalism at least in spaces that we control.

 # IDEAS FOR THE CLASSROOM

You will have your own preferences for how you create your seating plan. Gone are the days when you were required to hand in a seating plan, beautifully colour coded and annotated with every conceivable categorisation for each child in the room. Your seating plan should be for you alone (and your cover teachers) so that it is clear that you own the space and make decisions.

Your school may provide seating plan software for you. If it doesn't, there are free seating plan generators available online such as www.clickschool.co.uk and www.megaseatingplan.com that allow you to make seating plans quickly and neatly.

What you do once students are in a seating plan can be more important than actually creating one. While 'icebreakers' can make most of us want to crawl under a table, I would advocate their use in lower school, even if they result in something very simple – using names out loud that are unfamiliar and need to be pronounced carefully. Correct peer-to-peer mispronunciations with sensitivity.

(Continued)

Another point, often overlooked in the realm of classroom organisation is the issue of gender. Teachers who are initially unfamiliar with their classes sometimes default to 'boy, girl' seating. This can be difficult for students identifying, openly or otherwise, as transgender or non-binary. You may not see these identities straight away as a teacher, but avoiding 'boy, girl' seating is a starting point to make things a little less gendered in your space.

MANAGE YOUR INTERRUPTIONS

Unconscious bias, or implicit bias, is far more prevalent in our classrooms than conscious or explicit bias. Unconscious bias can be defined as a social stereotype formed of individuals or groups, based on, but not limited to, race, gender, sexuality, disability, class and age. Unconscious bias manifests far more frequently when we are under time pressure or managing lots of activities at the same time. It is hardly surprising, then, that the classroom is a fertile space for unconscious bias, particularly when it comes to gender.

In a groundbreaking study in 1975, Don Zimmerman and Candace West tracked the interruption rates in conversations between men and women. In the study, it was found that in same-sex two party conversational segments, the speakers had a near even rate of interruption and overlap. In cross-sex two party conversational segments, men accounted for 96% of interruptions (interjections that lead to the other person stopping the flow of talk), and 4% were attributed to women. 100% of overlaps (starting to talk before the other has finished) were attributed to men.

Interruptions are interesting interaction mechanisms. They serve to assert dominance and control in a conversation. Ask a Year 10 student how Lady Macbeth asserts her dominance over her husband in *Macbeth* and she will tell you that she interrupts and questions. It is ironic that she is seen as a manifestation of a witch for doing so and 'corrected' at the end of the play for her foolish attempt to control her husband and usurp the Elizabethan natural order. The rota fortunae turns. Exit Lady Macbeth. And yet we have a study here that shows that in our reality, mixed gender conversations are rife with interruption of girls and women.

REFLECTION

How confident are you in encouraging female voices in your classroom?

In the classroom, the phenomenon is replicated in teacher–student/student–student interactions. In *Still Failing at Fairness: How Gender Bias Cheats Girls and Boys in School and What We Can Do About It* (Sadker et al., 1994), the authors recount incidences of unconscious bias in teacher–student interaction, giving clear examples of how teachers are more likely to allow interruptions from boys, are more likely to allow boys to interrupt girls, and that without clear guidelines on managing these interactions, girls are less likely to speak up. Echoing this, in 2014, Kieran Snyder, a *Slate* journalist, wrote an article about gendered interruption rates. In 'Boys learn to interrupt. Girls learn to shut up', Snyder conducted a small scale personal study of gender disparities in discussion, revealing that boys were three times more likely to interrupt than girls in mixed gender groups. In girls-only groups, the girls interrupted each other more. Re-introduce boys, and girls stop interrupting.

The interesting takeaway from these pieces of research is that our unconscious bias allows gender inequality to take root. It is not just in interruptions that we see this pattern. How we allocate roles in class, our implicit ideas about what boys' needs are and what girls' needs are – all of these things serve to perpetuate gender roles that are reinforced over and over again in school and out of school as students grow older.

IDEAS FOR THE CLASSROOM

Good talk strategies have multiple purposes. The strategies below are common sense in a rigorous classroom that values oracy; they also serve to level the classroom in terms of unconscious inequalities:

(Continued)

- Consider carefully how you allocate talk partners – it should not be random.

- Teach students about the dynamics of talk – including gendered approaches to talk, without resorting to stereotypes.

- Allocate an observer in talk-based activities who monitors interruptions or dominance.

- Use the 'chip' strategy to include all voices. Give students an equal number of tokens they can 'spend' on contributions to a discussion. They have to use them all, but once gone, they cannot speak again. This levels the dominance in any group scenario. It's also effective in teacher meetings at all levels!

- Allow thinking and take up time to ensure that all students have time to gather thoughts.

- Use Doug Lemov's 'Cold Call' strategy to actively manage the range of responses you receive from the room.

- Actively bring attention to the negative effect of interruption between students.

WHAT ABOUT THE BOYS?

Even though, globally, boys have better access to education, the achievement gap in gender shows that boys do not perform as well as girls in secondary education in the UK. While there have been many attempts to close this gap, our understanding of teaching boys so that they perform as well as their female counterparts is limited. Who can remember being told that boys need to be more active in the classroom to succeed? That everything needs to be a competition? That we should accept shouting out because that's 'natural' to boys?

If you read only one book about boys' education and mental health, make it *Boys Don't Try: Rethinking Masculinity in Schools* (2019) by Matt Pinkett and

Mark Roberts. It is packed full of theory, personal experiences and current thinking about what it means to educate boys.

Gendered language can be hugely damaging to all genders. In your classroom and in your school, is gendered language common? It is worth tracking over the course of one day how many times you hear phrases such as 'man up' or 'boys will be boys' or 'I need two strong boys to move this table...'. A policy of not using those phrases in your classroom is a good starting point if there isn't already school policy on this.

INCLUSIVE SPACES

We tend to only consider the need for reasonable adjustments when we have students in our classroom with obvious, and by that I mean visible, disabilities. In these cases, one would hope that the child or children in question would have at the very least an IEP (Individual Education Plan) and at best an EHCP (Educational Health Care Plan) that outlines the adjustments that need to be made to ensure they reach their potential. Let's take hearing impairment as an example. In 2018, The Consortium for Research into Deaf Education found that 80% of deaf children were being taught in mainstream schools. They also found that there had been a 14% reduction in teachers for deaf students, with a 31% increase in deaf students needing support. It is not surprising that, according to statistics, deaf students are lagging behind their hearing peers in attainment and progress.

While we may not be specialists in teaching students with hearing impairments or any other disability, it is our responsibility to make sure we understand the basics of inclusive education. The first thing that needs addressing is our own attitude towards disability, visible or otherwise, something that UNESCO has flagged as part of their policy guidelines for inclusion, in which they state that schools have 'a responsibility to meet the diversity of needs of all learners, recognising that all children can learn' (UNESCO, 2009).

The suggestions below for creating an inclusive classroom are listed regardless of the established number of students with disabilities. The gold standard is to have a classroom that is sensitive to *potential* need; if you have students with hidden disabilities that have not been flagged as part of routine special educational needs provision, you are able to mitigate for disadvantage. It is always best to discuss special educational needs, identified or suspected, with your special educational needs co-ordinator.

Table 3.1 Supporting those with disabilities

Disability, impairment or need	Possible classroom issues	Inclusive practice
Autism/ASC	Noise sensitivity, sensory overload, turn taking in classroom discussion	Ear defenders allowed, classroom walls not overcrowded and bright, clear routines for talk; avoid 'functioning labels' such as high/low functioning that are packed with judgement!
Hearing impairment	Difficulty hearing instruction or information, echoing rooms, distracting noises	Seating plans with everyone facing the board; if known impairments, sitting in a location specific to hearing need, e.g. with back to a wall; all verbal communication from teacher given facing students. Videos checked for sound quality, subtitles used where possible.
Mental health-related disability	Trauma-related behaviours, compulsions, withdrawal, sensitivity to topics studied	Training on mental health related childhood behaviours, avoiding language that stigmatises mental health, e.g. 'that's mad' or 'I'm a bit OCD'; adapting 'zero-tolerance' strategies in the classroom – developing alternate strategies if necessary.

Disability, impairment or need	Possible classroom issues	Inclusive practice
Neural disabilities	Epileptic episodes (convulsive seizures and absence seizures)	Alertness for signs of both types of epileptic episodes, avoidance or pre-warning of flashing lights.
Visual impairment	Difficulty reading small text, undiagnosed short or long sighted, not able to access video resources	Font size at least 24pt on board; visualisers zoomed in; video accompanied by short verbal explanation; resources on A3; colour of paper considered.

Schools that genuinely embrace inclusivity are special places in which all teachers are made aware of how they can mitigate for needs arising from visible or hidden disabilities. These are the schools that know how to catch up a child with a disability that has been absent due to hospitalisation. These are the schools that understand some students do not want to talk about their hidden disability for fear of being 'different' or 'other', so disability awareness is built into everyday practice. These are the schools that say on entrance that they are inclusive and actually walk the walk.

NOTE IT DOWN

If you work in a co-educational setting, ask a colleague to observe your lesson with the sole purpose of examining and measuring interactions. You could provide them with a list of criteria to evaluate as they observe:

- Tallying responses from girls against responses from boys (where the respondee has been selected by the teacher)

- Tallying responses from girls against responses from boys (where responses are not cold-call)

- Tallying interruptions by gender

- Tallying teacher interruptions against gender (how many times you as a teacher interrupt the boys, or the girls)

- Tallying responses from each individual to create a mini-analysis of responses by gender, ethnicity, disability or SEND

It will not be possible to do all of these in one lesson!
However, if an objective observer provides you with the
data you need, consider the following questions:

1. Who talks most in my classroom considering the
   total percentage of boys and girls?

2. Who is 'missing' from the discussion?

3. Who does the interrupting in my classroom?

4. Am I reinforcing stereotypes unconsciously?

5. What can I do to resolve this?

CHAPTER 4
WHAT DOES A DIVERSE CURRICULUM LOOK LIKE?

This chapter covers:

- The importance of creating belonging through curriculum
- How you can meaningfully embed cultural connections into your curriculum
- How you can avoid 'victim narratives'.

DIVERSITY AND INCLUSION VS BELONGING

The Ofsted Inspection Framework highlights the need for schools to develop 'knowledge and cultural capital' (2019: 10) for all learners. Questions have been asked as a result of this. Whose culture? Whose knowledge? The arguments surrounding these questions could be debated for years; however, it seems to me that culture and knowledge should not belong to specific groups of people. Culture and knowledge can be far more democratic than that. By treating culture as something that exists in silos, we exacerbate an already pernicious issue – my culture is better than your culture, because we study it in school.

'The greatest good you can do for another is not just to share your riches, but to reveal to him his own.'
Benjamin Disraeli

In saying this, I argue that expanding the parameters of knowledge and culture is a far more effective way of bringing out community cohesion, whilst simultaneously developing stronger cognitive connections. This is where that wonderful word 'schema' comes in. Developing schemata, the sticking points for more knowledge to attach itself to, can only be a positive part of curriculum development. It is the difference between saying: *I know that mark making is important in art because Jackson Pollock was making marks in abstract paintings* and *I know that mark making is a universal human experience, and it goes back as far as the Lower Palaeolithic age, in the form of cupules, through the Lascaux cave paintings and Aboriginal art, to our modern day abstract paintings by artists such as Jackson Pollock.*

It is here that I defer to the work of Christine Counsell on curriculum design and knowledge. Christine has long been working on how we build schema, what knowledge is deemed important and how we go about giving students the broadest knowledge base to work from. She defines core knowledge as being 'like a residue' – the fundamentals of the curricular narrative. She goes on to add that with this core knowledge, we need a 'hinterland' of knowledge that acts to support the building of schemata (Counsell, 2018). One way of thinking about diversity in your curriculum is to work out what diversity looks like in both the core and the hinterland of knowledge for your subject.

By drawing together strands of global knowledge – either as core or hinterland, we are capable of creating what Pat Wadors, HR expert, called 'diversity, inclusion and belonging' (DIBs) in her fantastic talk *The Power of Belonging* (2016). She argues that we all want to feel that we belong – not that we are included as an afterthought.

The curriculum we deliver is the foundation of student knowledge. If that curriculum is limited to the thoughts, experiences, histories and achievements of white, western Europe, we are not allowing all students the chance to view the truth of the world they live in. We are not allowing them to build a wide enough schema to know they are citizens of the world and all of its history. Nor are we allowing them all to belong.

MATHS AND SCIENCE

The field of mathematics may not seem the most fertile when it comes to introducing cultural connections within the discipline. My favourite place to start comes in teaching about numbers themselves. I am reminded of a recent poll in the US, where 3,624 people were polled as to whether they wanted Arabic numerals taught in schools (Baynes, 2019). More than half (56%) responded that they did not want Arabic numerals in the curriculum. To be clear, the numerals 0, 1, 2, 3, 4, 5, 6, 7, 8 and 9 are what we call Arabic numerals. The poll response demonstrates to me that there is a fundamental lack of knowledge about the origins of numbers. There is space in the Mathematics curriculum to actively teach the development of numerical systems from the Indian subcontinent, through the Arabian world and into Western Europe and beyond.

A prime example of explicit teaching about origins of numbers lies in 'zero'. Various studies place the earliest recorded appearances of zero as Mesopotamian, Babylonian and even Ancient Mayan. It is now accepted widely that the predecessor of the modern zero was used as a placeholder in 5th–7th century Indian mathematics.

REFLECTION

How can I use homework, enrichment, after school clubs, and form time to add in global culture and history?

It seems vitally important to understand the global contribution to the development of zero. Without zero, we would not be living in our digital age – one that is predicated on the marked, binary existence of something and nothing. Even the language of zero creates cultural connection; the earliest word is *sunya* (Sanskrit), Arabian scholars called it *sifr*, Fibonacci called it *zephyrum*, Italians used *zefiro*, and it transcribed into English as *zero* in 1598. Its shape brings linguistic delight; *duck egg* and *goose egg* have been used as slang for zero, in tennis we called zero *love*, from the eggy French 'l'oeuf. Shakespeare contributes his standard bawdiness too; he refers to 'nothing' or 'o-thing' when hinting at female genitalia – which makes *Much Ado About Nothing* a far more interesting title for a play than you may have originally thought.

HISTORIES AND GEOGRAPHIES

The National Curriculum for KS1, KS2 and KS3 states as one of its aims that students should: 'know and understand significant aspects of the history of the wider world: the nature of ancient civilisations; the expansion and dissolution of empires; characteristic features of past non-European societies; achievements and follies of mankind.' This sounds wonderful as a starting point for a truly wide ranging, culturally connected history curriculum. When you read the curriculum for KS3, it is almost wholly dedicated to British history, apart from this tantalising snippet at the end, indicating that students should complete: 'at least one study of a significant society or issue in world history and its interconnections with other world developments [for example, Mughal India 1526–1857; China's Qing dynasty 1644–1911; Changing Russian empires c.1800–1989; USA in the 20th Century]' (Department of Education, 2013: 5).

Table 4.1 Evaluating your curriculum

	Half Term 1	Half Term 2	Half Term 3	Half Term 4	Half Term 5	Half Term 6
7	Ancient Egypt	Medieval life and living	How did the Renaissance change life and living?	Tudor and Stuart society	Victorian life	Change in the 20th century
8	The Normans	Church vs State (the Tudors)	Elizabeth I	Did democracy start with Cromwell?	The People and Political Power	The Empire – making Britain powerful
9	Medieval warfare	The development of the Navy	Revolutions	WW1	WW2	Cold War

It is undeniable that British history in Britain is necessary, just as American history in America, or Indian history in India would be. While we cannot ignore the mandated curriculum, we can carve space for narratives across the Key Stages that allow for cultural connections and representation.

Consider the History KS3 long term plan shown in Table 4.1.

In some ways, the sequencing of this curriculum is highly successful. It has a good sense of chronology, it revisits historical periods, it allows for greater depth of study as students go through the years. It is clear to see that there are opportunities for cross cultural connections to be made in the highlighted areas. They may be expanded on, as shown in Table 4.2.

Table 4.2   Adapting your curriculum

Ancient Egypt	Links to West African civilisations, the Benin Bronzes. Comparisons to the Assyrians (visit to the British Museum to evaluate symbols of power)
Did democracy start with Cromwell?	Proto-democratic societies (Sumerian), early democratic states in India, Ancient Greece/Rome
The Empire	Clear and sensitive representation of the impact of British colonisation on India/East Africa as well as domestic effects. Unflinching look at negatives for colonised populations as well as domestic advantages
Medieval warfare	Origins of gunpowder and weaponry, unbiased religious conflict in the Crusades
WW1 and WW2	Inclusion of soldiers from different cultures and contributions from the Commonwealth and Empire

The example above is a rough outline of some of the ways that diversity can be integrated. You may find other units of work that blend into that sequence of learning that open doors to diversity and inclusion. One thing is clear:

inclusion of global narratives alongside British history contributes to a greater sense of belonging and identity in students from different cultures, and also may contribute to a sense of how world cultures have shaped Great Britain.

After reading *The Good Immigrant* (Shukla, 2017), a collection of tales by people whose families have moved to Britain (and finding that my own questions and experiences were very much present in this text), the one historical subject area I would add to the History curriculum is 'migrations'. The power of tracing migratory history from the earliest invading forces through Huguenots, Jewish refugees, the Windrush migrants, migration from East Africa in the 1970s and so on would be enormous for students whose families may have been part of these international movements.

 ## CASE STUDY

Swerupa Gosrani teaches History at a school in Derbyshire:

In Year 7 we have included a unit on Plantagenet women, with the key question of 'How does power lie in female hands?' This is based on the ideas by Helen Castor and her book *She Wolves*. We also teach a unit on 'Black Tudors' based on the work done by Chris Lewis and Miranda Kaufmann's book. Within Year 8 we have used ideas that have come from the SHP 'Understanding History' textbook for Key Stage 3, published by Hodder Education, for example units on the sugar trade; migration through time to Britain; women getting the vote and rights, (this is based on the work done by suffrageresources.org); and the struggle for equal rights after the 1960s. For Year 9, when looking at WW1 we have tried to look not just at British soldiers, but also the role of women and Empire troops. We are also trying to use the 'meanwhile elsewhere' project to give students an insight into other places around the world.

TEXTS

With the politicisation of the English Literature curriculum, it is hard to avoid the implications of directing schools to focus on specifically British literature. For example, in the move towards a knowledge-rich English curriculum, there has been greater focus on literary antiquity. English departments across the country and indeed, internationally, are more likely to include epic and religious literatures of the white, western world into lessons designed to introduce students to the apparent beginnings of literature.

Of course, it is this concept that literature *begins* in Ancient Greece that may be problematic. A culturally connected curriculum strives to show connections in literature across the globe so that students have an understanding of how ideas, concepts and literary tropes are fantastically universal.

Take the concept of the hero. A knowledge-rich classroom may reference *The Iliad* and *The Odyssey* in the development of the hero. Perhaps then the teacher may introduce *Beowulf* as a literary development. What is missed is the global narrative of the hero. Epic literature exists universally, both in written form and in oral recount. In West African literature, the *Bayajidda* involves a hero slaying a serpent. In the *Ramayana* of India, Rama defeats the demon Ravana. In the epic of *Gilgamesh*, we have a king and his antagonist, a wild man called Enkidu. The duality here is a precursor for later texts that demonstrate the potential of the human soul to include the good and the evil. The Jekyll and the Hyde, in fact.

 ## IDEAS FOR THE CLASSROOM

The text matrix shown in Table 4.3 forms the basis of a unit on epic literature, focusing particularly on the formation of the hero, although the concepts of the monster and familial relations can be added. Ideally, it should be taught in KS3 to form a baseline for understanding protagonist and antagonist development. Because the texts will probably be in extract form, assessment

could be of locating information, inference and comparison, rather than specifically linguistic.

Table 4.3   Expanding the Literary Universe

The Epic of Gilgamesh (Mesopotamian)		
The Odyssey (European)	The Iliad (European)	Ramayana (Indian)
Beowulf (European)		
Sundiata (Malian)	Arthurian Legend (European)	

When planning the sequence of knowledge in English, providing a working baseline from which English literature springs is a beautiful way of creating a culturally aware classroom. This is a far better way to promote diversity than just choosing texts by BAME writers with no other purpose than to pay lip service to representation. When you choose texts, consider the 'lens' with which you are going to study the literature. When studying *Jane Eyre*, consider colonisation and representations of the 'other' in Bertha Mason; when studying poetry, choose poems that deal with disability, or sexuality. Diversity should not be limited to race and ethnicity in the English curriculum. It is also worth remembering that with non-fiction texts, the possibilities are endless.

These are starting points. There are infinite possibilities in the English curriculum to use, compare, analyse, and parallel texts from different cultures. The method of 'pairing' texts allows teachers to counter narratives on gender, race and sexuality, that in their contexts, may be at odds with current thinking in the 21st century.

ART AND DESIGN

Architecture is an under-studied topic in school. In reality, it is a cross-disciplinary and culturally connected topic that can be studied in DT,

Mathematics, Art and Religious Studies. Consider the dome of St Paul's Cathedral. Now compare to the Hagia Sofia of Istanbul and the Taj Mahal of India. Why does this shape hold design significance? Why is it significant in terms of religion? What came first? Who picked that shape and why?

The development of the house is another culturally connected field. Students can chart the earliest dwellings, evaluating their physical effectiveness, compared to Inuit abodes, Adobe huts, and then move on to modern architecture by Gaudi, Le Corbusier, Foster, and Zaha Hadid. Questions you might want to ask: how have different cultures adapted their homes to increase habitability? Which cities might have to adapt their architecture for their environment? How have modern architects learned from ancient cultures about buildings that last?

From an artistic perspective, it is worth looking at Angkor Wat's vast collection of carved external reliefs and whether there is anything similar in Western Europe. A comparison to the outside of Winchester Cathedral may help. An art project replicating design that is symbolic is a powerful activity that teaches students to plan, design, draw, replicate, adapt and evaluate.

 ## CASE STUDY

Claire Boreham teaches Art and Design Technology in a primary school for children with special educational needs and autism:

> **I'm trying to make sure the artists and designers studied are from a range of cultures, backgrounds and also that females are adequately represented. Yayio Kusama is a favourite as she's very accessible for my pupils and suffered a great deal of misogyny and mental health challenges in her life. I've regularly taught a Design Technology textiles project on batik using flour and water, inspired by a colleague who taught in South Africa for a number of years and by my own visit to Ghana. Batik can be linked to work on wax resist and screen printing.**

We look at the symbolism in Adinkra, and in traditional woven cloths which have symbolism based on pattern and colour, a little like tartan. Adinkra are linked to familiar logos and meaningful symbols we use in our day to day life.

NOTE IT DOWN

SELECT A SCHEME OF WORK, OR A SECTION OF YOUR SUBJECT LONG TERM PLAN. ANNOTATE IT TO FIND WAYS OF CONNECTING GLOBAL CULTURE, HISTORY AND EXPERIENCES.

AN EXAMPLE FROM SCIENCE:

Science topics	Possible diversity connections
Cells and non-communicable diseases	Henrietta Lacks, use of cells in cancer research
Cells and DNA	Rosalind Franklin, use of her research in structure of DNA
	James Watson's view on Eugenics
Space	Jocelyn Bell Burnell, Nobel prize controversy
	Lots of opportunities to present 'hidden figures' from Katherine Johnson to Mae Jemison
	Gallileo, blindness, theoretical physics
Atomic structure	Nuclear shell model proposed by Maria Goeppert Mayer
Radioactivity	Lisa Meitner, work on nuclear fission, and meitnerium named after her
Earth Science – structure of the earth	Inge Lehmann, Danish geologist who discovered earth has a solid inner core separate from a molten outer core

Topics **Possible diversity connections**

CHAPTER 5
HOW CAN WE CREATE GLOBAL CITIZENS?

This chapter covers:

- How privilege is relative
- How to create real world opportunities for students to understand cultures outside of their own to promote local/global understanding without a victim narrative
- How social justice is a concept that can begin in school.

Understanding your own privilege is a good starting point for teachers. It can be an uncomfortable process at first, as you have to examine the ways in which some of your inherited characteristics broadly mean that you have advantages that others don't necessarily have. In 1988, Peggy McIntosh, a Senior Research Scientist at the Wellesley Centers for Women, highlighted the relative privileges of being white and male in her paper *White Privilege and Male Privilege: A Personal Account of Coming to See Correspondences Through Work in Women's Studies*. In this, she wrote about 'unearned advantage' and how we can see this through the lens of race, sexuality, gender and physical ability.

'When we identify where our privilege intersects with somebody else's oppression, we'll find our opportunities to make real change.'
Oluo, 2018

Once we are aware of our relative privilege, what we do with it – and how we show our students the impact of that privilege – is of utmost importance. The most important aspects of understanding our own privilege are empathy, connectedness and allyship. Knowing that we have unearned advantages can help us to understand how to be an ally. Being an ally means understanding the ways in which you have privileges, and then working towards equity with the groups who have fewer advantages, without succumbing to saviourism.

GLOBAL CITIZENS

How do we teach our students to be true global citizens who are allies for those less privileged? Once your students know about their relative privileges, introduce your students to the concept of being a global citizen. Global citizenship can be defined as:

- Understanding the need to protect our environment and natural resources

- Standing up and speaking out against prejudice and injustice in all forms

- Taking action locally, nationally and globally on social and environmental issues.

 ## IDEAS FOR THE CLASSROOM

Instead of teaching students about poor working conditions in Bangladesh, a powerful alternative exists in showing students how their own consumption of goods has an impact globally.

Amy is 13 and lives in Manchester. She has to take a car to school because she lives so far away from it.

Salma is 13 and lives in Dhaka. The road to her school is closed because of flooding.

What are the connections between these two students? How does one life impact on the other?

How are these two students' lives connected? How does Amy's life impact on Salma?

The discussion around this activity is less centred on 'sympathy' for Salma, a Bangladeshi girl, but rather the impact of our own actions on her life. The intended endpoint is for students to understand that our consumption of resources and our actions on climate have an impact on people like us across the planet. There is no mention of her being poor or exploited as a premise in this activity.

THE SINGLE-STORY NARRATIVE PROBLEM

When it comes to education about the world we live in, teachers in schools do have good intentions. We signpost the world to our students; we introduce them to their global neighbours. Quite often, this is done via the means of assemblies or PSHE lessons. Consider this PSHE sequence of lessons on the topic of Conflict. Lesson 1 is an introduction to the topic of conflict. It starts with a sequence of images that students have to study to make connections. The images are taken from African nations that some of the students have never heard of: Sierra Leone, Somalia, the Sudan. The faces on the screen are predominantly black. Most of the faces are young. The lesson is on piracy off the coast of Somalia. The children learn there is a civil war and that Somalians commit violent acts against other Somalians and international vessels. Lesson 2 continues in a similar vein. This time, the topic is Sierra Leone and blood diamonds. Sierra Leone's children have guns. None of them are smiling.

Add this to images of Africa in assemblies when students are taught that in Africa, people are starving. That we need to give them money so they can survive. While we all know that famine, and war, and child soldiers are serious issues, reducing student exposure to just these aspects of the continent means that Africans – and by this I mean black Africans – are only ever perceived as criminals or victims. This is what is known as the 'single-story narrative'.

To combat this 'single-story narrative', other than having a curriculum that integrates diversity, we can start to show our students positive representations of global endeavour by BAME communities. There are countless examples of individuals and groups innovating to address issues within communities across the globe. Instead of seeing African faces as purely disadvantaged, in school assemblies, in form time, in citizenship teaching, present the engineers, the inventors, the social justice campaigners and politicians from those communities. Positive representation is possible.

UNDERSTANDING MICROAGGRESSIONS

In 1970, Chester M. Pierce coined the term 'microaggressions' when he noticed daily and commonplace verbal indignities, intentional and unintentional, being used by non-black Americans towards their black counterparts. These days, the term is applied to the commonplace verbal, non-verbal, intentional and unintentional insinuations and behaviours towards any marginalised group. It is a term that we may not be fully familiar with or have thought about before. Some examples of microaggressions might include:

- Deciding how 'bad' someone's disability is – 'You're lucky you only have X.'

- Assuming a person of colour was born outside of the country – 'Where are you from?'

- Assumptions about aptitude according to race – 'Your people are good at X, can you help me with X?'

- Assumptions about careers of people of colour – 'I'm surprised your father is a teacher, most people like you are X.'

- Using idiomatic language that contains offensive stereotypes – 'gyp', 'thugs', 'ghetto'

- Touching hair or clothes without permission, for example, asking black people if you can touch their hair, or adjusting a hijab

- Touching, adjusting or experimenting with equipment used to support a person with a disability

- Assuming all LGBTQ+ experiences are the same – 'You don't look gay...'.

It is important to teach students about microaggressions early, as, quite simply, they may not be aware of the negative impact of these interactions. Writing some common microaggressions down and matching them with possible interpretations and emotional impacts is a simple way to address them. Using restorative justice practice to explain why certain questions or assumptions are microaggressions is also powerful.

MAKING THE WORLD 'REAL'

International Exchange Programmes are becoming more and more rare in schools as budgets tighten and accountability measures limit student time outside of the academic curriculum. When I was at school, I had a French pen pal. Her name, as I recall, was Esther and we wrote to each other in halting English and French for a couple of years. Esther and I met when my school took a whole year group of students to France to meet our pen pals. Despite the awkwardness of meeting a virtual stranger, Esther and I spent time together getting to know each other and our respective cultures.

In many ways, I remember thinking that the experience for her meeting me was far more formative than the other way around. I was outside of her 'usual'. All of my schoolfriends looked so different from everyone in Esther's French town that we must have made quite the impression. I wonder if she, or her schoolfriends, ever spent as much time with a group of British Asians again.

'I am a citizen of the world'
Diogenes Laertius

If developing a pen-pal programme seems a little old-fashioned, you may want to consider inter-UK school exchanges, where students from your school spend time in a contrasting school for a short time. These experiences add value because they allow your students to exist in a different context and to meet people they might not readily meet in their 'home' environment. An important part of being able to empathise as an ally is to have a hands-on understanding of someone else's world. To be clear, this is not a vehicle for cultural or class tourism. Contrasting schools in partnership should have clear aims about collaboration, with guidance as to how student and teacher learning will be applied in the 'home' context.

In some ways, this is an attempt to recreate the experience of Derek Black, the subject of Pulitzer Prize winning journalist Eli Saslow's book *Rising out of Hatred: The Awakening of a Former White Nationalist* (2018). In it, Saslow provides an account of Derek's movement from being heavily allied to the Ku Klux Klan to being someone who understands, through first-hand connections and friends, the challenges that non-white peers face on a daily basis. The book highlights the need for people from different backgrounds to actually see each other, rather than know about each other's existence on the planet. In seeing and knowing someone who is different from you, there is a stronger chance of our students becoming allies with those who are different from them.

CASE STUDY

I watched the impact of introducing British students to a new culture first-hand a few years ago. In 2015, I was fortunate enough to work in a school that had an established exchange programme. I took four boys from inner city London – of Caribbean, Indian, African and dual Caribbean and white heritage – to an almost entirely ethnically homogenous place: Japan. For 10 days, four Year 10 boys lived with their Japanese families, went to schools in the Chiyoda district of Tokyo and lived, ate and breathed Japanese culture.

They were instantly aware of their difference in Chiyoda district. One of my students, 6ft in his socks and of Caribbean heritage, was stared at incessantly. In school, when Japanese students swapped their outdoor shoes for indoor slippers, there were none that fit my student's rather large feet. Whilst it was commented on politely, and with no little sense of wonder, by our Japanese hosts, my student was not made to feel excluded. It struck me just how different he must have seemed to our Japanese hosts and yet they did not treat him with disrespect, only with the reverence of any guest.

On the way home, we talked extensively about the difference between Japanese culture and our own British context. It fills me with pride to say that our conversation, even when we criticised a difference, was measured and full of understanding. It was a singularly powerful experience for those boys and for me.

NOTE IT DOWN

WHAT ARE YOUR PRIVILEGES? CIRCLE THE TERMS THAT DESCRIBE YOUR IDENTITY. CONSIDER HOW YOUR POSITION HAS AFFECTED YOUR ROLE IN SCHOOLS.

More Power	Bias	Less Power
Male	Androcentrism	Female
Masculine/Feminine	Genderism	Gender 'deviant'
White	Racism	Black/Minority Ethnic
European in origin	Eurocentrism	Non-European in origin
Heterosexual	Heterosexism	LGBTQ+
Able-bodied	Ableism	Disabled

(Continued)

Literate	Educationalism	Non-literate
Young	Ageism	Old
Attractive	Politics of appearance	Unattractive
Upper/upper middle class	Class bias	Working class
English-speaking	Language bias	Non-English speaking (EAL, not bilingual)
Light skinned	Colourism	Dark skinned
Non-Jewish	Anti-Semitism	Jewish
Fertile	Pro-natalism	Infertile

Source: Adapted from Morgan (1996)

CHAPTER 6
HOW CAN I HELP TO CREATE A DIVERSE CULTURE AT SCHOOL?

This chapter covers:

- How we can avoid a 'bolt-on' approach to diversity by 'usualising'
- How we can show outsiders our diversity values in the classroom and out of the classroom
- How we can influence positive change from our own level of leadership.

When considering how to help your school become more inclusive and diverse, there is no point just listing 'bolt-on' activities that sit outside of everyday experiences. Morgan Freeman famously once said that he considered Black History Month 'ridiculous' and some argue that confining the history of large groups of individuals to a mere month is insulting (Freeman, 2006). Rather than doing away with the idea completely, for it can be argued that these 'history months' are still needed while our curriculum lacks diversity, we should instead aim to shift the culture of our schools. The end point is to create a culture that acknowledges, values and celebrates diversity.

To be able to create a culture of diversity, the term 'usualise' is particularly useful. It is a term I first heard when I met Sue Sanders, the founder of Schools Out. She made it clear that the term was preferable to 'normalise', as the implication of normality is that there is a right way to be (*We are Family*, 2016). Normalisation, as a concept, was examined by Michel Foucault in his seminal work, *Discipline and Punish* (1975), in which he argued that 'normal' was used as a measure to exert social control. Those who fell out of the normative zone could be punished for it.

Using 'usualise' rather than 'normalise' allows us to convey the idea that there is an everyday-ness to diversity. It is not an add-on; it is the day-to-day reality of the world we live in. Explaining this to students is powerful. They will think in terms of 'normal' and 'not normal'. Imagine the possibilities that we open up for acceptance and celebration of diversity when we usualise what might be considered other by those who do not experience diversity very often.

REPRESENTATION MATTERS

One of the easiest ways to create a classroom that values and promotes diversity is to ensure that classroom and corridor displays are representative, regardless of the ethnic makeup of your intake. On one level, we are striving towards showing students who may be the minority in your school that they belong and are part of the fabric of the school. We are also showing *less diverse* intakes what diversity looks like in the rest of the world. This means that when we create displays about writers, scientists, mathematicians, doctors, lawyers, athletes, we show people of all backgrounds in those roles. It is important to consider display carefully; this means knowing what the stereotypes of various ethnically diverse peoples are. In one school I visited, I was really pleased to see that the PE department had displays that included BAME athletes. Except the rest of the school had no sign of any ethnic diversity on its walls. The message for students seemed to be that if you were black, you were destined to be a sportsperson.

> '*Design creates culture. Culture shapes values. Values determine the Future.*'
> Robert L. Peters

Walk down the corridors of any school and you will see the faces of former students and staff taking part in all sorts of activities. When schools are lacking in diversity in their own populations, it is doubly important that the very wallpaper of your school reflects a global social picture. Display is one of the easiest ways to 'usualise' difference. When was the last time you saw someone in a wheelchair in a display in school? Or anyone with a visible physical disability?

Think about the displays in your classroom and in your corridors now. You might already have a display that is ethnically representative. When was the last time you saw disability usualised in the classroom?

COLLABORATION WITH EXTERNAL BODIES

There are many organisations that support diversity and inclusion in schools. If you do not feel that your own experience as a teacher allows you to provide information and guidance to your students on disability, race, sexuality, gender and so on, it is worth seeking out external bodies that provide services for schools specific to those areas. The caveat on this approach is that often there can be a funding commitment; however, some organisations provide free services and advice (see Table 6.1).

Table 6.1   External organisations

Organisation	Area of expertise
Bemix	Learning Disabilities – provides workshops for students in schools to raise awareness of learning disabilities
Diversity Role Models	LGBT – provides links with role models who identify as LGBT+
Educate and Celebrate	LGBT – the Pride Youth Network supports young people in navigating their identity
Girl Up	Empowering girls – provides opportunities to develop confidence and leadership in girls
Holocaust Education Trust	Race – provides expertise in Holocaust education
JustDifferent	Provides disability workshops for primary schools
Mermaids	Gender diversity – the organisation supports schools, families and local authorities. There are resources to help train teachers on gender diversity on the website
Speakers for School	Inclusion – provides speakers from diverse backgrounds to visit schools
Stonewall	LGBT – teachers can undertake courses and lead their school towards becoming diversity champions

This is by no means an exhaustive list and is broadly UK specific; however, you do not have to go far to find advocacy groups for protected characteristics in your home country. Some organisations are local or regional and only work in specific areas. The list above is UK-based and national, with speakers who will travel to deliver workshops for your students, and serves as a starting point for your collaborative work.

 ## HINTS & TIPS

It is often said that there is not enough time to include workshops on diversity and inclusion. A little bit of creativity can go a long way in ensuring that your students have access to experts in diversity and inclusion. It is a requirement that schools provide spiritual, moral, social and cultural education in school settings. Some schools will do this through PSHE (Personal, Social and Health Education); however, as a teacher, you can ask to deliver an assembly using an external speaker. You can request that a group of students is taken off-timetable to take part in a workshop. You can engage students in the work of organisations such as Educate and Celebrate through extra-curricular clubs. One of my favourite ideas (not my own, I must add) is a Tea and Talks Lecture series, where visitors take tea with selected groups of students after school, and are able to discuss issues related to diversity and inclusion.

ASKING THE QUESTIONS

A school culture is not just about what we teach. The school culture is reflected in its staff body, its outward facing materials and its policies. As a staff member, asking questions of your school culture and curriculum is an important process, no matter what your role is. To help you get started in asking the right questions, take a look at the suggestions below:

1. What visible commitment does this school have to diversity and inclusion?

2. What does the website and prospectus tell me about the diverse culture of the school?

3. Are the values set out by the school, specifically around diversity and inclusion, lived through all policies, or just an act of lip service?

4. What does the application form and supporting material tell me about commitment to the Equality Act?

5. What does the curriculum include that shows a commitment to diversity and inclusion?

6. What does the wider curriculum commit to in developing a diverse culture?

7. How do policies support the experiences and backgrounds of all staff and students?

8. What do the physical spaces in school say about diversity and inclusion?

9. How do the governors support the need for a diverse and inclusive curriculum and school environment?

10. How are the community/parents and/or carers involved in building a diverse culture?

Whether you are applying for a post at a school, already work there, or are involved in its leadership and governance, these questions serve as a starting point for discussions. Schools in which this questioning is commonplace make changes to their daily practice that have profound effects on student experience.

 HINTS & TIPS

Below are some suggestions for actions that could be taken to ensure diversity is embedded within your school's culture and practices:

- Ensuring there are gender neutral toilets and changing spaces available and that there isn't an onerous process to access them

- Challenging gendered language across the whole staff body through staff training

- Reviewing the curriculum so that is it robust and diverse

- Displaying commitment to diversity in outward facing spaces such as reception

- Developing a diversity and inclusion policy that holds people to account

- Partnering with diversity-based organisations to deliver staff training

- Adapting school uniform and policy

- Delivering assemblies on diversity and inclusion

- Evaluating your displays and website for implicit messages sent about intake and staff body, as well as visitors.

FINAL WORDS

Wherever we are in our understanding of diversity in schools, there is always more to be done. From the simple act of educating oneself and enacting that learning through our interactions with students, to building diversity into the fabric of what we teach, and indeed, the whole school culture, we are taking steps to address a pressing need.

There will never be a magic well of time for teachers to dedicate themselves to this endeavour. We do make time for what we value. It is with that statement that we should consider what, as teachers, we want to dedicate our time to.

Whether you are able to take a small step or a large step towards developing a school culture that values diversity is not important. *Taking the step* is important. It might be something you do in your own classroom, a tiny change in the way you speak or present course materials. It might be in the questions you ask of your students. It might be in the discussions you have with your staff teams.

It comes back to the idea of creating connections. Perhaps you are one of the diamonds holding together Indra's net. You reflect the lives and experiences of all others in the way you choose to teach. You create the conditions in which all children, from all backgrounds, are seen and valued.

NOTE IT DOWN

CREATE AN ACTION PLAN. USING THE TABLE BELOW, PLAN OUT YOUR FIVE PRIORITIES NOW THAT YOU HAVE READ THROUGH THIS GUIDE. WHAT STEPS WILL YOU TAKE? WHO WILL YOU NEED TO TALK TO?

	Action	Resources
1		
2		
3		

(Continued)

4

5

CHAPTER 7

WHERE CAN I FIND SOURCES OF INFORMATION AND SUPPORT?

This chapter covers:

- The power of networking to ensure that you stay up to date with diversity and inclusion work
- The essential books you need to develop your own understanding of diversity and inclusion.

THE POWER OF NETWORKING

My own experience in meeting people who are passionate about diversity and inclusion comes from Twitter. I joined nearly ten years ago and found myself networking online, engaging in discussions about gender, race and identity with like-minded people who wanted to bring diversity into the discussion in schools. I was fortunate enough to 'meet' the steering group of @WomenEd, a wonderful group of women who were starting the conversation on women's visibility in education. Through my engagement with WomenEd, I met the founders of @BAMEedNetwork, another group of educators who were tackling the lack of BAME teachers in educational leadership. I went to their conferences, I met even more like-minded folk. From there stemmed my engagement with @LGBTedUK. The work of these organisations was brought together when Hannah Wilson, former headteacher and diversity champion, created @DiverseEd2020.

'Keep your language. Love its sounds, its modulation, its rhythm. But try to march together with men of different languages, remote from your own, who wish like you for a more just and human world.'

Camara, 1971: 61

On your own, you can only do so much. By networking with groups such as these, you gain a sense of collective agency. The support for creating diverse schools is out there. You only have to scratch the surface of social media to find organisations and teachers who will give you ideas and advice.

THE DIVERSE SCHOOL READING LIST

This reading list is both a guide to current essential thoughts on diversity and a starting point for further exploration. These choices do not necessarily mean they are the definitive representation of any given topic, only a part of the discourse on diversity and inclusion. If I have mentioned a text in the main body of this book, I may not have re-listed it here, unless I feel it is necessary.

DISABILITY AND BODIES

- Elizabeth Barnes, *The Minority Body: A Theory of Disability*
- Jonathan Bryan, *Eye Can Write*
- Robert McRuer, *Crip Theory: Cultural Signs of Queerness and Disability*
- Katharine Quarmby, *Scapegoat: Why We Are Failing Disabled People*
- Tom Shakespeare, *Disability: The Basics*

COLONIALISM, POWER AND IDENTITY

- Franz Fanon, *The Wretched of the Earth*
- Michel Foucault, *Discipline and Punish*
- Pankaj Mishra, *From the Ruins of Empire*
- Edward Said, *Culture and Imperialism*
- Edward Said, *Orientalism*
- Ngugi Wa Thiong'o, *Decolonising the Mind*

GENDER

- Melissa Benn, *What Should We Tell Our Daughters?*
- Kate Bornstein, *Gender Outlaw*
- Betty Friedan, *The Feminine Mystique*
- Audre Lorde, *Sister Outsider*

- Janet Mock, *Redefining Realness*

- Grayson Perry, *The Descent of Man*

- Matt Pinkett and Mark Roberts, *Boys Don't Try: Rethinking Masculinity in Schools*

- Susan Stryker, *Transgender History*

MENTAL HEALTH

- Lisa Appignanesi, *Mad, Bad and Sad: A History of Women and the Mind Doctors from 1800 to the Present*

- Clare Erasmus, *The Mental Health and Well-Being Handbook for Schools*

- Nathan Filer, *This Book Will Change Your Mind About Mental Health*

- Nicola Morgan, *Blame My Brain*

- Bessie Von Der Kolk, *The Body Keeps the Score*

NEURODIVERSITY

- Barb Cook and Dr Michelle Barnet, *Spectrum Women: Walking to the Beat of Autism*

- Jon Donvan and Caren Zucker, *In a Different Key: The Story of Autism*

- Temple Grandin and Richard Panek, *The Autistic Brain*

- Eva A. Mendes and Meredith R. Maroney, *Gender, Identity, Sexuality and Autism*

- Dr Barry M. Prizant, *Uniquely Human: A Different Way of Seeing Autism*

RACE AND ETHNICITY

- Akala, *Natives*

- Robin DiAngelo, *White Fragility*

- Reni Eddo-Lodge, *Why I Am No Longer Talking To White People About Race*

- Afua Hirsch, *Brit(Ish): On Race, Identity and Belonging*

- David Olusoga, *Black and British*

- June Sarpong, *Diversify*

- Nikesh Shukla, *The Good Immigrant*

- Garth Stahl, *Identity, Neoliberalism and Aspiration: Educating White Working-class Boys* (Routledge Research in Educational Equality and Diversity)

- Beverly Daniel Tatum, *Why are all the Black Kids Sitting Together in the Cafeteria?*

SEXUALITY

- Meg-John Barker, ill. Julia Scheele, *Queer: A Graphic History*

- Allan Bérubé, *Coming Out Under Fire: The History of Gay Men and Women in WW2*

- Michel Foucault, *The History of Sexuality*

- Graham Robb, *Strangers: Homosexual Love in the 19th Century*

- Siobhan B Somerville, *Queering the Color Line: Race and the Invention of Homosexuality in American Culture*

- Tea Uglow, *Loud and Proud: LGBTQ+ speeches that empower and inspire*

REFERENCES

Aberjhani (2009) *The Bridge of Silver Wings 2009*. Lulu.com.

Baynes, C. (21 May 2019) 'Most Americans say "Arabic numerals" should not be taught in school, finds survey', *The Independent*, 21 May. Available at: www.independent.co.uk/news/arabic-numerals-survey-prejudice-bias-survey-research-civic-science-a8918256.html (accessed 14 October 2019).

Baynton, D. (1998) *Language Matters: Handicapping an Affliction*, Disability History Museum. Available at: www.disabilitymuseum.org/dhm/edu/essay.html?id=30 (accessed 12 January 2020).

Benedict, R. (1934) *Patterns of Culture*. New York: Houghton Mifflin.

Camara, H. (1971) *Spiral of Violence*. London: Sheed and Ward.

Counsell, C. (2018) 'Senior Curriculum Leadership 1: The indirect manifestation of knowledge: (A) curriculum as narrative', in *The Dignity of the Thing*, 7 April [blog]. Available at: https://thedignityofthethingblog.wordpress.com/2018/04/07/senior-curriculum-leadership-1-the-indirect-manifestation-of-knowledge-a-curriculum-as-narrative/ (accessed 19 December 2019).

Department of Education (2013) *History Programmes of Study: Key Stage 3*. Available at: https://assets.publishing.service.gov.uk/government/uploads/system/uploads/attachment_data/file/239075/SECONDARY_national_curriculum_-_History.pdf (accessed 12 June 2019).

Diogenes Laertius (1979) *Lives of Eminent Philosophers II* (R.D. Hicks, trans). Cambridge: Harvard University Press.

Fosslien, L. and Duffy, M.W. (2019) *No Hard Feelings: The Secret Power of Embracing Emotions at Work*. New York, NY: Penguin.

Foucault, M. (1975) *Discipline and Punish*. London: Penguin.

Freeman, M. (2006) *Freeman on Black History*. Available at: www.cbsnews.com/video/freeman-on-black-history/ (accessed 17 May 2019).

Jourard, S.M. (1971) *Self-disclosure: The Experimental Investigation of the Transparent Self*. New York: Wiley.

McIntosh, P. (1988) *White Privilege and Male Privilege: A Personal Account of Coming to See Correspondences Through Work in Women's Studies*, Working Paper 189. Wellesley, MA: Wellesley Centers for Women.

Morgan, K.P. (1996) 'Describing the Emperor's new clothes: Three myths of education (in)equality', in A. Diller, B. Houston, K.P. Morgan and M. Ayim, *The Gender Question in Education: Theory, Pedagogy & Politics*. Boulder, CO: Westview.

Ofsted (2019) *Education Inspection Framework 2019: Our Rationale, and How it Will Work in Practice*. Available at: https://assets.publishing.service.gov.uk/government/uploads/system/uploads/attachment_data/file/772056/School_inspection_update_-_January_2019_Special_Edition_180119.pdf (accessed 24 November 2019).

Oluo, I. (2018) *So You Want To Talk About Race*. New York: Seal Press.

Pierce, C. (1970) 'Offensive mechanisms', in F.B. Barbour (ed.), *The Black Seventies*. Boston, MA: Porter Sargent.

Pinkett, M. and Roberts, M. (2019) *Boys Don't Try: Rethinking Masculinity in Schools*. Abingdon: Routledge.

Sadker, D., Sadker, M. and Zittleman, K. (1994). *Still Failing at Fairness: How Gender Bias Cheats Girls and Boys in School and What We Can Do About It*. New York: Scribner.

Said, E. (1993) *Culture and Imperialism*. London: Chatto and Windus.

Saslow, E. (2018) *Rising out of Hatred: The Awakening of a Former White Nationalist*. New York: Penguin Random House.

Shukla, N. (ed.) (2017) *The Good Immigrant*. London: Unbound.

Snyder, K. (2014) 'Boys learn to interrupt. Girls learn to shut up', *Slate*, 14 August. Available at: https://slate.com/human-interest/2014/08/child-interruption-study-boys-learn-to-interrupt-girls-as-young-as-4-years-old.html (accessed 21 May 2019).

Soroff, J. (2014) 'The eyes have it', *The Improper Bostonian*, 23 May. Available at: https://www.colorlines.com/articles/uzo-aduba-never-thought-about-changing-her-nigerian-name (accessed 13 January 2020).

Tatum, B.D. (1997) *Why are all the Black Kids Sitting Together in the Cafeteria?: And Other Conversations About Race*. New York: BasicBooks.

UNESCO (2009) *Policy Guidelines on Inclusion in Education*. Available at: https://unesdoc.unesco.org/ark:/48223/pf0000177849 9 (accessed 14 April 2020).

Wadors, P. (2016) *The Power of Belonging*. Available at: www.youtube.com/watch?v=xwadscBnlhU (accessed 14 October 2019).

We Are Family (2016) 'Up close and personal with Sue Sanders, founder of LGBT History Month', *We are Family*, 15 February. Available at: https://wearefamilymagazine.co.uk/up-close-and-personal-with-sue-sanders-founder-of-lgbt-history-month/ (accessed 2 March 2019).

Wright, H. (2012) 'City of London Boys' School headmaster compares segregation in London's education system to "apartheid-era South Africa"', *The Independent*, 11 September. Available at: www.independent.co.uk/news/education/education-news/city-of-london-boys-school-headmaster-compares-segregation-in-londons-education-system-to-apartheid-8125909.html (accessed 14 April 2020).

Zimmerman, D.H. and West, C. (1975) 'Sex roles, interruptions and silences in conversation', in B. Thomas and N. Henly (eds), *Language and Sex: Difference and Dominance*. Stanford, CA: Stanford University Press, pp. 105–129.

INDEX